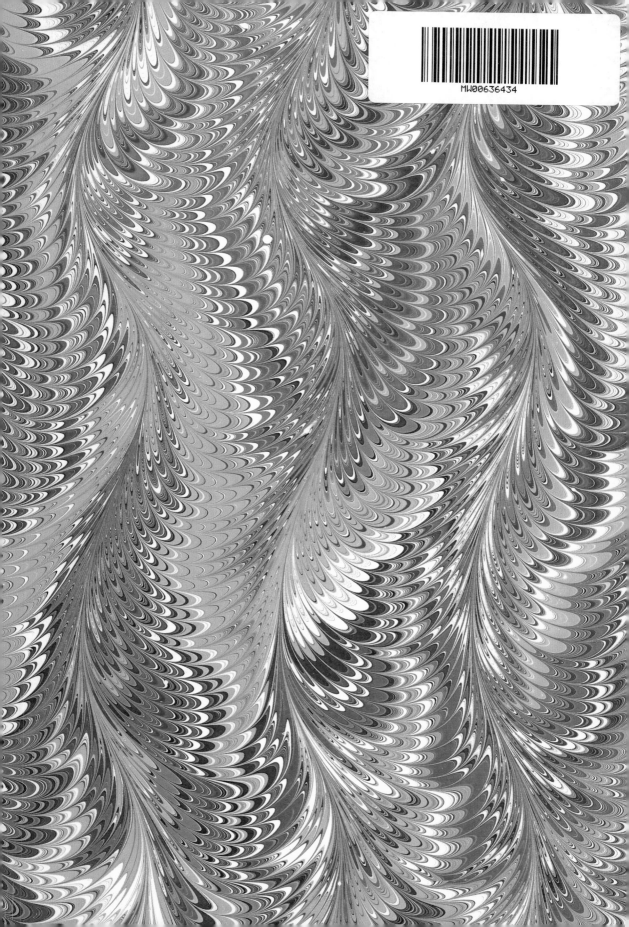

German Combat Engineers
in World War II
1939-1945

Schiffer Military/Aviation History
Atglen, PA

Translated from the German by Ed Force

Copyright © 1998 by Schiffer Publishing, Ltd.
Library of Congress Catalog Number: 98-84757

Printed in China.
ISBN: 0-7643-0574-3

This book was originally published under the title, *Deutsche Pioniere im Einsatz 1935-1945 Eine Chronik in Bildern* by Podzun-Pallas.

We are interested in hearing from authors with book ideas on related topics.

Published by Schiffer Publishing Ltd.
4880 Lower Valley Road
Atglen, PA 19310
Phone: (610) 593-1777
FAX: (610) 593-2002
E-mail: Schifferbk@aol.com
Please write for a free catalog.
This book may be purchased from the publisher.
Please include $3.95 postage.
Try your bookstore first.

Horst Riebenstahl

German Combat Engineers in World War II

1939-1945

A Photo Chronicle

INTRODUCTION

By far the great majority of the photos shown here were taken by members of the former engineer troops. A few show technical faults, yet on the other hand they are not posed photos, but genuine action photos of particular expressive power.

In this volume of pictures—simply for lack of space—diagrams of unit structures, equipment statistics, etc., of the individual engineer troop units have been omitted. Within the large area of "crossing bodies of water", the Weapon Arsenal volumes "Military Bridgebuilding Materials of the Wehrmacht" and "Assault Boats of the German Engineers 1934-1945" are recommended.

PODZUN-PALLAS-VERLAG

ACKNOWLEDGMENTS

We would like to thank the engineers themselves and the widows of fallen comrades, whose support contributed to the existence of this photo documentation. In particular: W. Ackermann, K. Ahlbach, J. Eidam, H. Kreckmann, A. Kuhn, M. Lehr, K. Röder, F. Rudolph, O. Schmidt, H. Speck, H. Steuer and Th. Vogt.

SOURCES

Federal Archives (BA)
Central Archives of the Engineers
Podzun-Pallas-Verlag Archives
Riebenstahl Archives
Scheibert Archives
and all the persons named in the acknowledgments.

CONTENTS

A bridge over the Meuse, built by engineers of the 7th Panzer Division in 1940.

FOREWORD

The German engineer troops developed out of a branch that only developed into a fighting service arm by World War II. Thus in addition to the special engineers, there also arose designations such as assault engineers, armored engineers, etc. The last war demanded a tremendous lot of these troops in terms of technical ability and the combat involving it, what with the technology that developed more and more quickly.

From this wide field, the volume at hand shows approximately 300 protographic documents, most of them never before published—including rare photos of bridgelaying tanks in action, mine removal, and the unimaginable construction of makeshift bridges.

It was possible to gain outstanding support from former engineers of all ranks, so that I was able to assemble several hundred original photos and put this volume together. I would especially like to call attention to the mine-listening company, a special unit for clock-regulated radio remote-control ignition over great distances. The bridge over the Asopos (in Greece) with its pillars ninety meters high is also of particular interest.

All in all, a pictorial volume such as never before existed for this multitalented service arm has come into existence.

Under cover of fire, the engineer shock troop sets out across a body of water in rubber boats.

1939

Practice with a half-pontoon of Type B bridge material. With this equipment, not only ferries but also eight-ton bridges up to 83 meters long, or 16-ton bridges up to 54 meters long, could be built.

This is a finished eight-ton bridge of Type B material. This is also a photo of training shortly before the 1939 Polish campaign.

Auch hier wird ein Halbponton bei einer Übung zum Brückenbau an das Gewässer getragen (Gewicht 750 kg).

Here too, a half-pontoon (weighing 750 kg) is being carried to a body of water as part of bridgebuilding training.

A photo from peacetime.

Assault boats being put into the water under cover of a smoke screen (in training, as the fatigues show).

An assault boat shortly before it "jumps" into the water. The group leader is in front, the boat's motor to the left.

On September 2, 1939, the second day of the war, an Opel Kapitän drives across a swampy brook that has been made passable by planking.

Hier wird ein Panzer I des Panzer-Regiment 1 der 1. Panzer-Division auf einer 16 t-Ganzponton-fähre von Pionieren des Panzer-Pionier-Bataillon 37 über die Weichsel gesetzt.

Here a Panzer I tank of Panzer Regiment 1 of the 1st Panzer Division is being taken across the Vistula on a 16-ton whole-pontoon ferry by men of Panzer Engineer Battalion 37.

On many advance routes, bomb craters were found by the troops. Engineers were sent in at once to make the roads driveable for the following troops. September 1, 1939, the first day of the war.

At the edge of a village in Poland on September 1, 1939, some of the barricades have been pulled loose by tracked vehicles (tanks) using cables.

Panzer engineers are placing explosive charges to remove barricades in Poland in 1939.

The Klobuk railroad bridge, blown up by the Poles, was later put back into service by German engineers.

Wood for the construction of corduroy roads is being gathered and sorted, probably a training measure.

And here horsedrawn wagons must be led over a quickly laid corduroy road, Poland 1939.

Here a motorized column is driving slowly over a corduroy road laid by engineers.

Round lengths of wood are laid as a corduroy road at each end of a newly-built bridge in 1939.

An SPW of a company of Rifle Regiment 1 of the 1st Panzer Division traverses swampy meadows in Poland in 1939. The men of Engineer Battalion 37 had their hands full making the terrain passable, using boards, fences, long and short poles.

A makeshift crossing helps traffic over a shell crater.

A shock troop crosses a Polish river on a rubber-raft footbridge in 1939.

An eight-ton B-material bridge is built over the Bug south of Brest-Litovsk near Vlodava in 1939. Because of low water, the bridge rests on nine trestles. From the middle section on, it is a K bridge, consisting of two end-pieces.

A bridge over the Warthe, blown up by the Poles, is made passable for German infantrymen.

A bridge of various types of timber, built by the men of Engineer Battalion 62, is weight-tested with a Panzer II in Poland in 1939.

Repairing a wooden bridge near the Liswarte in Poland, September 1939. Here braces are being added to the bridge's piles.

This pile bridge was built by engineers in 1939.

The wooden bridge in Panki, blown up by the Poles, was repaired by the men of Panzer Engineer Battalion 37.

This bridge over the Liswarte was partly destroyed by the Poles. Here units of the 1st Panzer Division ford the river with their Krupp trucks in September 1939.

A wooden bridge, blown up by the Poles, is examined in view of rebuilding.

A bridge over the Buzzara, also blown up by the Poles. It too was rebuilt by German engineers.

A military trestle bridge of B material in September 1939. The trestle legs, spars and braces (three braces each) can be seen clearly.

An eight-ton tractor pulling a heavy howitzer through a ford located by engineers. Measuring poles mark the entrance of the land bridge.

At left is a 16-ton military bridge of B material, crossing the Vistula near Annapol in 1939. At right, a heavy bridge is being built to replace it.

A military bridge over the Vistula in Poland, built of B material in 1939. Because of the low water level, the bridge rests on twenty trestles.

Infantrymen and engineers set out across the Vistula in Poland in 1939.

A Vistula bridge in Poland, built by German engineers in 1939.

There were many barricades in Poland. Thanks to the engineers, most of them could be removed or opened quickly.

Soviet troops west of Brest-Litovsk, Poland, in 1939. On the German side were engineers of Panzer Engineer Battalion 39.

1940

Like all other troops of the Wehrmacht, the engineers used the time between action in Poland and France for training. Here they are using an assault boat.

And here they are using a loaded A-material ferry to transport a 20 mm Flak gun.

The Wittenberg engineers train at a landing on the Elbe. Here a link between a land bridge and a B-material ferry is just being built. The floating part of the bridge is lower, so a ramp section (the angled part) was built.

M-boats have propelled the ferry across the Moselle. Sixteen-ton ferries carry Panzer III of the 1st Panzer Division.

Panzer Engineer Battalion 37 practices using K material on the Moselle before the 1940 French campaign. The lattice carrier on the left is already in place; that on the right is just being pushed over the roller by the engineers, using an extender trestle. At left is General Kirchner, 1st Panzer Division.

This wagon carries K material. The end pieces with the roller trestles above them can be seen. Winter 1939-1940.

A K-material bridge built on the Moselle before the 1940 western campaign by Panzer Engineer Battalion 37. The extender trestle can be seen; the men practice pushing the carrier over the rollers.

The engineers of the 1st Panzer Division build a bridge on the Moselle before the 1940 western campaign, practicing with K material. Three lattice carriers, combined to make a 16-20-ton bridge, can be seen.

A K-material bridge built on the Moselle in 1940 by Panzer Engineer Battalion 37 of the 1st Panzer Division. The extender and roller on the carrier end can be seen.

Pieces of B material are being carried across a river on floats.

Divers are checking the utility and effect of bridge pillars while clearing the riverbed of the Moselle in March 1940, before the French campaign.

Die Einsätze in den Niederlanden, Belgien und Frankreich (1940) verlangten unzählige Brückenbauten aller Art. Hier ein 16 t-Übergang über die Maas bei Sedan. Mehrere Brückengeräte B, gebaut vom Korps Pi.-Btl. 62.

Action in the Netherlands, Belgium and France in 1940 required countless bridges of all kinds. Here a 16-ton bridge, built by Corps Engineer Battalion 62 of much B material, crosses the Meuse near Sedan.

This 16-ton bridge was built near Nouzouville.

Diese 16 t-Brücke wurde bei Nouzouville geschlagen.

A 16-ton whole-pontoon bridge crosses the Aisne near Chateau Porcien, France, in 1940.

A sixteen-ton bridge at Amiens in 1940.

Ready for a crossing on rubber rafts at Zutphen, Holland, in 1940.

A bridge over the Issel, blown up by the Hollanders, before being put back into service.

Crossing the Meuse at Maastricht in 1940.

Crossing a rubber-boat bridge near Dinant, France, in 1940.

Here is a very makeshift footbridge, with ladders to the other shore.

An 8-ton B-material bridge over the Meuse near Dinant, May 1940.

A first makeshift crossing next to a blown-up bridge.

46

Barricades are removed by engineers so the infantry can advance.

Barricades removed by engineers near Juniville, June 1940.

47

Everything was thought of, even taking along suitably cut boards to turn a railroad line into a roadway, making the line passable for motor vehicles.

Boats guard the Rhine crossing at Grossenbraisach in 1940.

Men of Panzer Engineer Battalion 37 of the 1st Panzer Division after taking the fortress of Belfort, June 1940.

Street barricades in Martenlange are removed.

Engineers bring vehicles across the Meuse near Dinant, France, on an eight-ton double ferry.

Building a trestle bridge over the Semois in Bouillon.

A bridge column with B equipment drives over a makeshift bridge.

By the Rhine-Marne Canal near Minencourt, engineers remove a street barricade.

A horsedrawn l.FH 18 crosses a military bridge in France in 1940.

Engineers drive to a bridge site with their bridgebuilding materials.

Parts of Rifle Regiment 1 cross a bridge, built by engineers, over the railroad lines at Sedan in May 1940.

A 16-ton whole-pontoon bridge of B material, built by Engineer Battalions 37 and 505, over the Meuse near Sedan, France, in May 1940.

A motorboat of Panzer Engineer Battalion 37 of the 1st Panzer Division (note the symbol on the bow) is launched from a trailer at Gravelines in 1940. It had a 6-cylinder, 100 HP Maybach motor and was used to push and pull ferries and build bridges.

Engineers examine a blown-up bridge near Maastricht in 1940.

Repairing a bridge, with components ready to be erected.

Railroad engineers restore destroyed rail lines in Amiens in 1940.

Infantrymen cross the Rhine on a large pontoon bridge in 1940.

Moving the heavy Flak artillery was often difficult. Here a camouflaged gun is moved across an eight-ton (B material) bridge over the Dise near Sarron, France, in 1940.

Electromagnetic minesweepers are used to locate metal mines.

A shell crater, filled with rainwater, in a road near Kure, France, in 1940.

The struggle to deal with obstacles often demanded great sacrifices of the engineers, as did their dangerous work with mines and explosives.

Ready to attack, the men lie under their assault boats near Colmar on the upper Rhine during the 1940 western campaign.

The command to attack has been given. Lightning-fast, the assault boats are pushed into the water.

The shore behind them is hidden by fog, so that the enemy has a hard time seeing the preparations for the assault; France, 1940.

A boat assault on the Rhine.

The boats have landed. Now to establish a bridgehead. 1940.

Weapons and vehicles are ferried across the Seine on rubber rafts; France, 1940.

Engineers bring the shock troops and their weapons across the river in rubber rafts.

Engineers use their mine-locating poles in Belgium in 1940.

Only the pole helps to find nonmetallic mines. Here engineers look for French mines in a village in 1940.

French mines are removed near Mauberge.

Building a K-bridge. The box carrier and the extender with a roller at its end are seen clearly.

A Panzer III tank with a swastika on its turret (for air identification) crosses the Aisne on a 16-20-ton pontoon bridge.

Engineer equipment trailers of Panzer Engineer Battalion 37 stand on a square in burning Bouillon in May 1940.

In Gravelines (near Dunkerque), chaos prevails on the streets in May 1940.

On the Salm, near Trois Ponts, the enemy blew up the big railroad and highway bridges. The rails hang in mid-air as the only remaining link, while engineers build a military bridge.

In the background is the blown-up bridge. In front of it, engineers have built a 16-ton K-bridge. In the foreground, a makeshift bridge is being built.

Rubber rafts cross the Ghent Canal in Belgium in 1940.

A Panzer III with corduroy road and smoke cartridges on the rear rolls across a K-bridge over the Sure at Bodagne, Belgium, in 1940.

This bridgelaying tank on Panzer II chassis, seen in France in 1940, did not work well and was later replaced by Type F 14.

Engineer battalions and army angineers were often called on to build corduroy roads.

Another 1940 photo from France shows a bridgelaying tank on Panzer II chassis, carrying makeshift fast-bridge parts.

When the western campaign ended, intensive training of newly drafted soldiers began, using some nerly developed equipment. Here the Corps Engineer Battalion is on the Vistula with motorboats, assault boats and rubber rafts.

Whoever could not work on the boats strengthened himself—probably not willingly—with gymnastics.

Crossing a river—here on rubber rafts—under enemy fire in Belgium in 1940.

Another training picture—they didn't use trumpets in combat. Blowing up ruts had to be practiced too.

In order to construct an eight-ton bridge, much practice, measuring and other work of all kinds were needed.

H
s
R

1941

This is one of twelve assault-footbridge tanks built by Magirus on Panzer IV chassis. It was capable of laying an infantry footbridge up to 26 meters long. It saw service in Russia in 1941.

der Masse von Magirus stammenden Sturmstegpanzer auf dem Panzer IV-Fahrge-
ge, einen Infanterie-Sturmsteg in einer Länge von 26 m abzusetzen. Er kam 1941 in

Here a K-bridge is being erected as a reviewing stand in Allenstein, East Prussia, before the 1941 eastern campaign. A 16-ton K structure is being combined with two middle and two end pieces plus ramps. The plank covering is being added below.

Here the carrier beams are being placed on the trestle spars. The shore beam, the right trestle leg and the footplate, as used on land bridges, are seen at the bottom of the picture.

Another view of the reviewing stand in Allenstein, East Prussia. An engineer is working on the trestle winch lock and chain, part of the 8-ton B material.

Here we see the land bridge with a trestle brace and rail, of the reviewing stand in Allenstein, East Prussia.

In the reviewing stand in Allenstein, we see an eight-ton bridge being built of B material. Schoolboys and youths are quite interested. A trestle brace runs diagonally through the middle.

A sixteen-ton whole-pontoon bridge, linked to a land bridge by a ramp. Trucks with assault boats cross the military bridge over the Luga, built by Corps Engineer Battalion 62 in the summer of 1941.

An eight-ton tractor and boat trailer drive across a twelve-ton bridge, strengthened with double planks, the trestles also strengthened with two braces. The rail clamps set in the underpinnings can be seen clearly.

A crossing of logs and other wood, 1941.

Weight testing by an eight-ton tractor, 1941.

Building a swamp causeway, 1941.

A footpath has been built quickly by putting planks over remaining bridge pillars, 1941.

An infantry footbridge, quickly built of planks, 1941.

Footbridges could be prepared in advance, finished or cobbled up; this one uses rubber rafts.

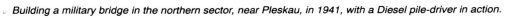

Building a military bridge in the northern sector, near Pleskau, in 1941, with a Diesel pile-driver in action.

A land bridge of K material serves as a landing stage for K-material ferries on the Duena near Jakobstadt, June 1941.

A rubber-raft ferry sets out across the Duena in the area of the 1st Panzer Division west of Jakobstadt in the summer of 1941.

A bridge over a water-filled ditch near Wyasma on the 1941 advance route.

Horsedrawn artillery crosses a trestle bridge in Russia in 1941.

A trestle is erected to support the middle of a bridge in 1941. The footplates at the bottom and trestle braces at the top provide the necessary support.

A bridge over the Jura near Tauroggen, blown up by the Russians; beside it, the trestle bridge built by Panzer Engineer Battalion 37.

A B-material trestle bridge, with the trestle legs supported by two braces, and the spars and other members, plus the underpinnings with clamps holding the double roadway, easy to see.

The shore timbers are in place, with the trestle and footplate in the background and the spar linking the two trestle legs.

A land bridge is being built at Luga by Corps Eng. Batt. 62 in the summer of 1941, with the carriers from the land (shore timbers) to the trestle (spar) easy to see. Each trestle leg is supported temporarily by one brace.

A bridge of B material with a land bridge at Luga in 1941. Note the buffer that links the ferries with the 16-ton whole-pontoon bridge.

A Panzer III of the 2./Kp. Pz. Regiment 1 crosses a trestle bridge that has been strengthened with a doubled roadway.

Artillerymen pull their gun across a trestle bridge spanning the low water of the Duena in 1941.

A trestle bridge with double roadway crossing the Luga, built by Panzer Engineer Battalion 37 in July 1941.

A trestle bridge in Russia, seen in 1941.

In the background, a makeshift bridge is being built; in front of it is a trestle bridge built by an engineer battalion, to be dismantled when the bridge in back is finished.

SPW mit 3,7 cm Pak des Pz.Grn.Rgt. 113 fährt
über eine 16t K-Brücke. Stützweite 14,40 m bei Ein-
bau von zwei Endstücken und einem Mittelstück in
jeden Träger.

An SPW with 37 mm Pak of Panzergrenadier Regiment 113 drives across a 16-ton bridge with a span of 14.40 meters, plus two end pieces, with a middle section in each carrier.

Panzer Engineer Battaliin 37 has built a bridge of 16-ton K material and corduroy roadbed near Wyasma in late September 1941. Transition rails have been laid over the logs and timbers.

A military bridge of K material, with a Panzer III crossing the Beresina in 1941.

A 16-ton bridge with a double trestle supporting the middle. The joint has been covered with transition rails. An eight-ton tractor and boat trailer are being used to test its load capacity. Russia, 1941.

A road bridge over the Velikaya near Ostrov, Russia, blown up by the Russians, in the summer of 1941, replaced by Panzer Engineer Battalion 37 with two K materials, a middle and two end pieces, and crossed by Artillery Regiment 73 vehicles in the summer of 1941.

K material in use in Russia in 1941.

A 16-ton K-material ferry with two middle sections and two end pieces (19.2 m long) crosses the Duena.

Building a bridge over the Luga in Russia, summer 1941.

A 16-ton K-material bridge in the Velktye-Luki (Vitebsk) area, winter 1941. The two end pieces for a 16-ton K-material bridge, and the approach rails, are easy to spot.

A K-material bridge with transition rails laid on the end pieces (pressure places) in 1941.

A bridge over a tank ditch on the Stalin Line, built by engineers in 1941. A B-material trestle forms the middle, with two trestle braces and approach rails on each side.

A Tatra truck and boat trailer of the II. Bridge Column of Panzer Engineer Battalion 37, 1st Panzer Division, in the summer of 1941.

A whole-pontoon ferry is made of B material and taken to a 16-ton bridge on the Duena in the summer of 1941.

A bridge position is prepared on the Luga in the summer of 1941.

An eight-ton tractor with pontoon trailer crosses a ford, discovered by engineers, on its way to the next bridge position in the summer of 1941.

A 16-ton B-material bridge is crossed in the summer of 1941.

Building a 16-ton whole-pontoon bridge. The land bridge, trestle legs, braces and spars are easy to see. A 16-ton bridge required 12 carriers and a double roadbed.

A 16-ton whole-pontoon bridge is being built of B material, crossing the Luga, in the summer of 1941.

A 16-ton whole-pontoon bridge of B material required twelve carriers and a double roadbed. Here two p[...] are being linked.

Engineers had to do heavy work, often under enemy fire.

A 16-ton whole-pontoon bridge over the Luga in 1941.

A Panzer III crosses a 16-ton bridge of B material, built by Panzer Engineer Battalion 37. The floating par bridge are linked to the sloping banks with transition rails. Russia, 1941.

A 20-ton whole-pontoon bridge, one of those over the Duena near Jakobstadt, had to rest on six trestles because of low water. Rails link the bridge with the shore. Summer 1941.

A makeshift bridge with reinforcements, built by Corps Engineer Battalion 62.

A makeshift bridge over the Duena at Welisch in 1941. On it is an s.J.G. 33 of the 1st Panzer Division.

A large makeshift bridge in Smolensk in 1941.

A bridge collapses under a Panzer III in Russia in 1941. Tank crews remove the wreckage.

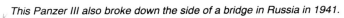

This Panzer III also broke down the side of a bridge in Russia in 1941.

An eight-ton tractor and boat trailer cross a makeshift bridge through the Stalin Line west of Ostrov in the summer of 1941.

A makeshift bridge built by Corps Engineer Battalion 62 near Pleskau, Russia, in 1941; note the side rails.

A makeshift bridge built with B material, crossed by Tatra and Krupp trucks and an eight-ton tractor in the winter of 1941.

The same bridge, with a trestle and two braces. At right are several pyramidal antitank teeth of the Stalin Line.

A company chief drives over a bridge built by his men, to test its strength, in Russia in 1941.

The railway engineers had to do hard work to make destroyed bridges usable again. Here they are driving piles for a bridge in Russia in 1941.

A railway bridge blown up by the Russians in 1941, being restored by railway engineers using a Diesel pile-driver.

Railway Engineer Regiment 4 building a railway bridge near Kovno in 1941.

Here supports for the superstructure of a railroad bridge are being built. Makeshift pyramidal structures are being used.

The makeshift railroad bridge at Kovno stands. The engineers have done a tremendous job, and the weight test is completed.

The men of Regiment 4 pose for a souvenir photo and hang on the bridge like grapes on a vine.

Men of Corps Engineer Battalion 62 arrive to build a bridge west of Ostrov in the summer of 1941.

The bridge column of Corps Engineer Battalion 62 is on its way to Pleskau in the summer of 1941.

Towing tractors pull equipment trucks, while motorcycle messengers are stuck in the mud. Swamps and shallow waterways made building bridges difficult. Russia, July 1941.

Through the lattice one can see the bridge built over a Russian tank ditch near Vyasma in 1941.

This bridge at Pleskau was blown up by the Red Army in the summer of 1941.

This SPW (Sd.Kfz. 251/1) has launchers attached. The soldiers called it the "Stuka on Foot" or the "Howling Cow" because of the powerful effect of, and the noise made by, the 28- or 32-cm grenades it launched.

Hier ein SPW (Sd.Kfz. 251/1) mit angebrachtem Wurfrahmen. In der Landsersprache hießen sie auch »Stuka zu Fuß« oder »Heulende Kuh« wohl wegen der starken Wirkung der 28 bzw. 32-cm-Wurfgranaten und des heulenden Abschußgeräusches (BA).

A "Stuka on Foot" with loaded launchers in Russia in 1941.
Below: The SPW launches a grenade.

Above and below: An engineer SPW with attachments for launchers so they could also be set up away from the vehicle. They were still launched from the SPW. Note the lower picture on the next page. (BA)

This SPW, with a rack for 28-, 30- or 32-cm grenades (Stuka on Foot), is moving to a new position in Russia in 1941.

A grenade is being fired in Russia in 1941.

Capable mechanics of the 13th Panzer Division have attached a launching rack to a Skoda 38(t) tank.

Here a grenade is being launched from the 38(t) tank in 1941. 28-cm (50 kg of explosive), 30-cm (with explosive or incendiary oil) or 32-cm (50 kg of oil) grenades were used.

The assault-boat pilot was always a member of the engineer troops.

Assault boats cross the Dniepr at high speed south of Mogilev, Russia, in 1941.

Assault boats cross the turbulent Wuox, a river near Viborg, Finland, in 1941.

South of Mogilev, Russia, infantry and engineers cross the Dniepr on rubber rafts in 1941.

A damaged road bridge is reinforced in the Leningrad area in 1941.

A corduroy bridge over swampy terrain near Ostrov, Russia, in 1941.

A burning bridge is being dealt with in Russia in 1941.

Restoration of a railway bridge at Kovno, blown up by thew Russians, begins in 1941.

On many lines the Russians blew up the rail joints, which had to be adjusted to standard gauge by railway engineers.

A scouting troop of railway engineers leaves its railcar (in the background) to examine a destroyed railroad bridge.

Russian mines.

Only the minesweeping rod helped to find metallic mines. Sidearms were used if needed. Many engineers lost their lives thereby.

Russian mines are being removed at the edge of a village.
Below: A Russian "coffin mine" is being defused in 1941.

Construction in the winter. In the vastness of Russia, the winter made heavy demands on the soldiers. Raised bunkers required strong logs.

Men of Engineer Battalion 62 build a bunker outside Leningrad in 1941.

Heavy burdens often had to be carried.

A makeshift bridge has been set afire by an air attack. The men try to put out the fire with extinguishers while going on with their repair work.

Engineers of the LAH use concentrated charges in an attack on the Stalin Line in 1941.

An SPW of Panzer Engineer Battalion 37 is being relaired outside Leningrad in 1941.

A bridge over a brook near Velikiye-luki, with two shore beams at each end, carriers, underpinnings with clamps plus carriers and a log roadway, crossed by trucks with motorboats in 1941.

When they retreated across the Dniepr, the Soviets had no time to blow up the bridge across the river. Only later in 1941 did gunboats and aircraft tri to destroy the bridge.

A camouflaged house as a Stalin Line bunker. A German assault engineer studies the burned-out concrete block with interest.

A K-material bridge of two middle and two end pieces, plus pontoon support, in Latvia in 1941.

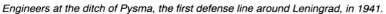

Engineers at the ditch of Pysma, the first defense line around Leningrad, in 1941.

1942

Above: A 251/5 in Russia; below, one rolls along the French Riviera. Both photos were taken in 1942.

Um die Jahreswende 1941/42 kamen die Pionier-Schützenpanzerwagen (Sd.Kfz. 251/5 und 251/7) verstärkt in die Panzer-Pionierbataillone. Sie sind gekennzeichnet durch eine Kastenreihe oberhalb der Kettenabdeckungen und durch eine »Sturmbrücke« rechts und links vom Kampfraum (BA).

As 1941 turned to 1942, the engineers' Schützenpanzerwagen (Sd.Kfz. 251/5 and 251/7) reached the armored engineer battalions in greater numbers. They are recognized by a row of compartments above the track aprons, and by an "assault bridge" on each side of the fighting compartment. (BA)

The upper photo was taken in training; the lower one shows an engineer Schützenpanzerwagen of the GD Division.

A bridgelaying tank on Panzer IV chassis (see next pages) drives across a bridge laid by another tank in 1942.

A bridgelaying tank on Panzer IV chassis approaches its destination in 1942.

Brückenlegepanzer auf Fahrgestell des Panzer IV fährt zum Einsatzort, 1942.

A bridgelaying tank platoon on its way to a readiness point, following a Panzer I to protect the bridge, in the summer of 1942.

The footbridge could be extended like an extending ladder. The bridge was 26 meters long and weighed some 50 m/kg. Below: a 26-meter bridge in position, being crossed by the infantry.

This truck and pontoon trailer of Panzer Engineer Battalion 37 were destroyed by low-flying Russian planes in 1942.

This truck and boat trailer, of the same battalion, were destroyed by low-flying Russian IL II at Rshev in 1942.

Ferries made of rubber rafts and B material are in action on the Ossuga in Russia in 1942.

An eight-ton bridge of B material crosses the Dniepr in 1942.

A 16-ton B-material bridge is being built across the lower Don near Kourtafinka in July 1942.

A military bridge is crossed by an SPW of Rifle Regiment 1 of the 1st Panzer Division in Russia in 1942.

The very versatile mountain bridging material is used here as a cable footbridge in 1942.

Heavy vehicles of Artillery Regiment 73, 1st Panzer Division, use a ford, next to which is a rubber-raft bridge for light vehicles, in Russia in 1942.

Here two sets of K material, with two middle sections, middle support and approach rails made a bridge 38.4 meters long across the Stoss in 1942.

A KW 1 has broken through this bridge over the upper Donetz near Voronesh in 1942.

After part of this bridge was blown up, the turret of the KW 1 can still be seen in the water. A K-material span has been built.

This bridge near Roslav was blown up by the Russians in 1942. Wood for rebuilding is already on hand.

In the background is a 16-ton bridge of B material at Bruisk, Ukraine. In the foreground, Engineer Battalion 45 is driving piles with a ram to build a makeshift bridge.

This road bridge over the Beresina was built by Corps Engineer Battalion 62 in 1942.

A heavy bridge is being built over the Beresina in 1942. Prepared nail-carriers are being installed. They were used when boards were used in place of heavy beams or steel members.

A company's equipment and supply trucks drives over a small makeshift bridge in the winter of 1942.

A makeshift bridge over the Vasusa, near Szytchevka, Russia, in the spring of 1942. The driven piles are ready for a second roadway.

A pile bridge with 5-meter spans and braces, in the central sector of Russia in 1942.

THE ENGINEER LISTENING COMPANY

This special unit of the German engineer troops, hitherto quite unknown, was organized in the autumn of 1941 by Engineer Training Battalion z.b.V. (for miners) in Höxter on the Weser, after important buildings had been destroyed by mine explosions, at first unexplainable, in large cities like Kharkov lying well back in the hinterlands. Their task was the precise location and removal of the Russian charges. Technically, this was a complete surprise. At first it was suspected that the equipment came from America.

The company consisted of three platoons (1 officer, 4 NCO, 40 men), each composed of four listening troops. The 1st Platoon (Oblt. Dietrich) served with Army Group North and was to remove mines from Leningrad, among other cities. The 2nd Platoon (Oblt. Oster), with Army Group South, served in Rostov, Sevastopol and Krasnodar; the 3rd Platoon (Lt. Pohlmann) saw its last service and met defeat in Stalingrad.

The large Russian mines (up to 1000 kg), with remote control by radio, were designated the F-10 Device. Wooden crates weighing 25 kg, filled with small bags of explosive, were linked together in at least three places in the foundation and secured against removal by pull fuses. Charges in bags had their fises hidden in the igniter.

The eight-tube radio set with built-in electric clock (using minimal current) and the 12-volt battery (accumulator) were packed in a watertight rubber bag, likewise equipped with a pull fuse.

To receive the ignition signal, a wire antenna, 20 to 30 meters long, was laid under the street pavement, or in the building under decorations or tiles. The antenna was always the indication of a large remote-control mine. When being removed, this was immediately shortened piece by piece, in order to weaken the reception of the ignition signal. Tips about antennae also came from nervous civilians, from whom the installation had not been concealed. To keep the F-10 Device ready to receive signals for at least three months, the electric clock of the receiver switched to reception for some eight seconds every three minutes. Every receiver was tuned with a tuning fork to a certain wave length and height for separate ignition, as soon as the occupation of the building by staffs or offices was reported by agents.

The charges and rubber bag (ignition device) were connected by hidden wires. With the so called "listening grenade", a metal cylinder 40 to 50 cm long, with a built-in crystal microphone planted about half a meter in the ground, attempts were made to locate the quiet electric switching clock, which was successful only very close.

Between the microphone and the usual headphones there was a battery-powered intensifier.

As long as the triggers (with their pull fuses) were not removed from the battery in the rubber bag, this work was life-threatening.

The ignition devices remained ready to work for some three months. During this time they could be activated from up to 300 km behind the front line. One such large mine in Kharkov killed General Georg von Braun, a cousin of the renowned rocket-builder Wernher von Braun, and other officers.

One of the last living eyewitnesses, Uffz. Friedrich Rudolph, was a troop leader in the 2nd Platoon of the Engineer Listening Company. He was flown out of the Kuban bridgehead during the German retreat in a Ju 52 supply plane with freight gliders, in order to rescue this small special troop. Further action out of Höxter was seen with the XXXVI Mountain AK in Lapland.

A reporting post for radio mines, in both German and Russian, was set up for civilians' use. Rex, a German Shepherd of the 2nd Engineer Listening Platoon, examines the signs.

An opened rubber bag with five ignition cables, radio receiver (left) and connected battery (right). The rubber bag was secured with pull igniters.

A watertight rubber bag with five ignition cables, and its radio receiver (left) and battery with electric cable (right) already removed. Pull igniters secured the bag where it was closed.

A Russian eight-tube radio receiver for remote-control mine ignition, effective several hundred kilometers away (very rare photo marked TOP SECRET).

A rubber bag with radio receiver, battery and electric clock, plus a 25-kg charge, all installed. The power cables can be seen by the bag and on the wall.

The igniters are already defused, and the 25-kg boxes of explosive are being removed from under a large public building. The troop leader of the 2nd Platoon is Uffz. Friedrich Rudolph.

At an Italian support point at the east end of the Corinth Canal, in Greece, engineers build a bridge of new J material (for heavy bridges up to 80 tons) in 1943.

1943-1945

Ein BL IV s (Sturmstegpanzer) fährt über die Kriegsbrücke in Bobruisk.

A BL IV s (assault-bridge tank) crosses the military bridge in Bobruisk.

Panzer Engineer Battalion 37 of the 1st Panzer Division practices using J material near Sparta, Greece, in 1943.

Men of Panzer Engineer Battalion are ferried at Sparta in 1943.

Here Panzer IV tanks of the 2nd Panzer Regiment of Panzer Division 1 are ferried to Euboea in 1943.

*Ab 1943 kam der »Leichte Ladungsträger Goliath«
bei der Pioniertruppe zum Einsatz. Über Kabel
ferngesteuert, brachte er Sprengladungen in gegne-
rische Stellungen. Hier ein »Goliath« mit Elektro-
motoren, die in späteren Produktionen durch Ver-
brennungsmotoren ersetzt wurden.*

As of 1943, the "Goliath Light Load Carrier" saw action with the engineers. Cable-controlled, it moved explosive charges into enemy positions. Here is a Goliath with electric motors, which were replaced by internal combustion engines in later production.

The Goliath in action.

Members of the U.S. forces examine captured Goliaths on the invasion front in 1944.

Ferries of J material cross a river with heavy weapons (Hummel and short SPW) of the 1st Panzer Division. Above, a ferry is being built out of J material.

Road and footbridges built at Lissjanke Nord.

An infantry footbridge in the Tcherkassy pocket in February 1944.

An engineer SPW with T-mines hung on the sides.

This flamethrowing SPW ran afoul of a mine.

An SPW as a medium flamethrowing vehicle. The men wear seldom-worn protective clothing above; below is a practice session.

Armored flamethrowing vehicles of the 1st Panzer Division could throw a flame 60 to 70 meters for up to 1.5 minutes.

Bei den deutschen Pionieren gab es ab 1942 verschiedene Flammpanzerwagen. Am zahlreichsten vorhanden und bis Kriegsende vertreten war der hier und auf weiteren Seiten gezeigte Flammpanzerwagen (Sd.Kfz. 251/16).

From 1942 on, the German engineers had various flamethrowing vehicles. Until the war ended, the type used in greatest numbers was the Flammpanzerwagen (Sd.Kfz. 251/16) shown here and on the next pages.

Two practice photos of Sd.Kfz. 251/16 with the new (angled rear) SPW body.

Above, another practice photo; below, an action photo from Russia in 1944.

Here lies part of the three-section bridge over the Asopos (on the Greek line from the North to Athens) blown up by the British in 1943.

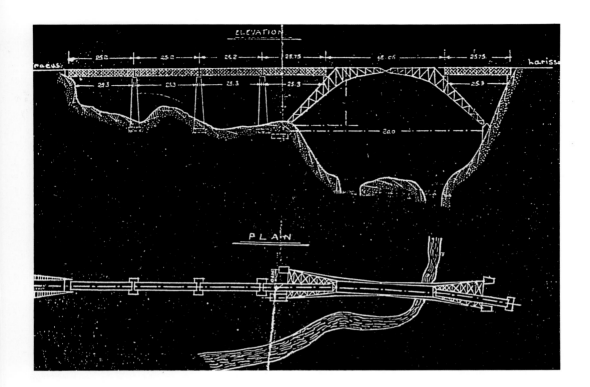

FATEFUL BRIDGE

This bridge over the Asopos on the rail line from northern Greece to Athens came into German hands unharmed. About two years later, on June 21, 1943, at 2:15 PM, the bridge was blown up by a British command landed by parachute.

Railway engineers worked at top speed to rebuild it. Shortly before the work was finished, a hydrauilc lifter failed, the superstructure slid, fell off and buried Construction Chief Major Siebert and 27 men under it.

But the bridge had operational importance. Railway engineers went to work on it all over again and did the job quickly. The pillars, 90 meters high, were made of Roth-Wagner material. The superstructure, with roadbed on top and two-story open approaches on both sides, had one ballast carrier on each side.

Particular difficulties: no approach roads, just footpaths. Tunnels on both sides of the bridge, with slopes and curves.

Major Siebert and 27 NCO and men died a soldier's death in this terrible accident.

"By hand, meaning with compressed-air hammers, picks and shovels, the non-supporting rock is removed so the concrete foundation for the Roth-Wagner bridge pillars can be laid."

Obgfr. Martin Lehr of the measuring troop of Railway Engineer Company 63 (inset) was injured by falling bridge pieces.

Railway Engineer Company 63 is seen rebuilding the railroad bridge over the Save near Belgrade in the summer of 1944, using Roth-Wagner material.

There were no limits to the creative ideas of the German engineers, particularly for makeshift bridges and fast repairs. This destroyed railroad bridge near Vygonotchi (Kursker Bogen) was made usable in only three days by German engineers, using countless sills to make a "sill-stack bridge".

A railroad bridge near Lvov, blown up by the Russians in 1944.

Repairs begin on a road bridge near Lvov, damaged by enemy aircraft, in 1944.

From footbridges (above) to B-material bridges (below, an 8-ton bridge over the San) and makeshift bridges of all kinds, these jobs, along with many others, were the main activities of the division engineer battalions—and often done under enemy fire.

Honors, but death as well, came to the German engineer troops in the years from 1939 to 1945.